TEAM SPIRIT!™

BAND FRONT
COLOR GUARD, DRUM MAJORS, AND MAJORETTES

Jason Porterfield

Bethel Middle School
Media Center

rosen
central™

The Rosen Publishing Group, Inc., New York

Published in 2007 by The Rosen Publishing Group, Inc.
29 East 21st Street, New York, NY 10010

First Edition

Library of Congress Cataloging-in-Publication Data

Porterfield, Jason.
Band front: color guard, drum majors, and majorettes/
Jason Porterfield.—1st ed.
        p. cm.—(Team spirit!)
Includes bibliographical references (p.) and index.
ISBN 1-4042-0729-5 (library binding)
1. Marching drills. 2. Drum majorettes. 3. Marching bands. 4. Color guards. 5. Drum majors.
I. Title. II. Team spirit! (New York, N.Y.)
GV495.P67 2006
784.83—dc22

                                                                    2006004496

Manufactured in the United States of America

On the cover: The Lane Tech High School color guard leads the marching band in the annual Columbus Day Parade in Chicago, Illinois.

CONTENTS

SILKS AND TWIRLS

The music is audible in the parade long before the marchers come into view. When the crowd finally catches sight of the band, the first impression is of smartly spun silks (flags), the glint of twirling batons, and the choreographed dance routines of the pom squad. The band front presents a dazzling visual accompaniment to the rousing music.

Whether it's the Macy's Thanksgiving Day Parade or a small-town Fourth of July parade, the band front puts on a stirring display that leaves audiences cheering. The band front performs for various spirit-raising events. High school and middle school groups demonstrate their routines in rallies, halftime shows at sports

Members of the color guard are scattered among the musicians of the Pella Community High School marching band from Pella, Iowa, in this formation during the school's presentation at the Rose Parade Band Fest in Pasadena, California, on December 30, 2002.

events, and parades. College and professional groups perform in spectacular halftime shows in front of tens of thousands of spectators and a television audience. The best baton twirlers, color guards, and pom squads take the spotlight in public venues such as Disney World or Las Vegas shows. Performers at all levels show off their skills in competitions sponsored by national organizations.

Band front has its origins in military demonstrations. Today, pageantry has added theatrical and artistic elements to the original martial displays. Also known as "the performing arts," pageantry blends dance, costume, theater, and music. Instead of hailing triumphant armies returning from war, modern pageantry groups celebrate sporting events and national celebrations. However, teams and individuals are increasingly being recognized as main events in shows and competitions.

Participation in band front requires time, dedication, skill, and teamwork. However, the reward is well worth the hard work. Teams experience the exhilaration of performing before cheering crowds. Outstanding performances can bring not only personal satisfaction but also awards and even scholarships. Most important, band front participation forges friendships, teaches the importance of teamwork, and creates happy memories that will last a lifetime.

CHAPTER 1

What Is Band Front?

Band fronts present visual spectacles during marching band performances and competitions. Their routines combine dance, gymnastics, and props. The components of band front vary from group to group, but they generally include a color guard, a drum major, majorettes, and a pom squad.

The introduction of a band front to marching bands in the United States began in the late nineteenth century.

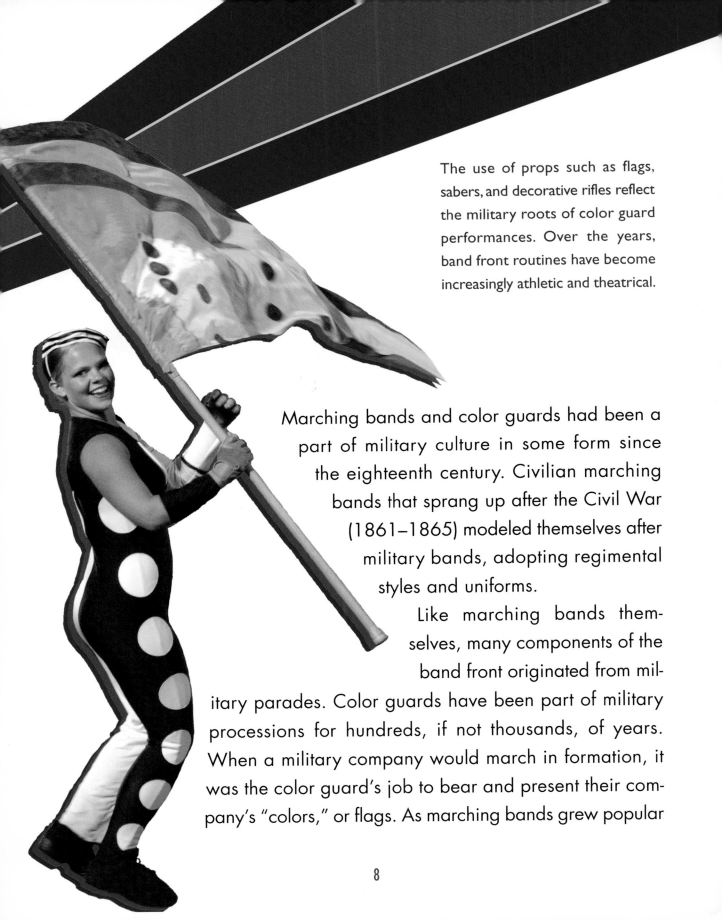

The use of props such as flags, sabers, and decorative rifles reflect the military roots of color guard performances. Over the years, band front routines have become increasingly athletic and theatrical.

Marching bands and color guards had been a part of military culture in some form since the eighteenth century. Civilian marching bands that sprang up after the Civil War (1861–1865) modeled themselves after military bands, adopting regimental styles and uniforms.

Like marching bands themselves, many components of the band front originated from military parades. Color guards have been part of military processions for hundreds, if not thousands, of years. When a military company would march in formation, it was the color guard's job to bear and present their company's "colors," or flags. As marching bands grew popular

The U.S. Naval Academy Color Guard presents the colors in the opening ceremonies of an Army vs. Navy football game at the Lincoln Financial Field in Philadelphia, Pennsylvania.

during the late nineteenth century, military color guards would march with civilian bands while the bands played patriotic songs. They would present their flags at parades and athletic events. The rifles and sabers used by color guards serve as reminders of their military origins.

During the 1920s, color guards started holding flags belonging to different nations while marching in formation with the band. Crowds reacted enthusiastically to the varied flags. Soon, color guards began using colorful, non-representational flags and orchestrating shows around their presentations. The interest in color guards grew with the popularity of college sports, particularly football. By the 1930s, color guards had a presence in many college marching bands. High school color guards followed suit.

Twirling has evolved into a challenging skill that requires overall coordination as a group as well as precise hand-eye coordination from each individual.

Majorettes' participation in marching bands dates back to just after the end of the Civil War. According to one popular story, the term "majorette" was first used by Major Reuben Millsaps, a Civil War veteran who founded Mississippi's Millsaps College in 1889. He named the female athletes—including baton twirlers—at his new college the Majorettes, after his rank in the Confederate army.

Baton twirling itself originated from early drum majors, who would toss their conducting batons into the air during performances. These early batons were heavy, awkward pieces of carved wood used by drum majors to keep the marching band in time. As batons became lighter, more women joined and led marching bands, in many cases replacing drum majors. Crowds at parades and sporting events enjoyed watching the twirling routines. By the 1930s, majorettes and their twirling routines were regular features of most band performances. The first formal baton twirling associations were formed during the 1950s, eventually leading to the establishment of the United States Twirling Association (USTA) and the National Baton Twirling Association (NBTA).

Pom squads are one of the most recent additions to the band front. Cheerleading at sporting events dates back to the 1880s, but it wasn't until the invention of pom pons in the 1930s that they became part of the band front.

Color Guard

Color guard performances often leave audiences dazzled and cheering. Throughout the year, millions of people see color guards dancing and spinning their flags and other props, either in person or on television. Their costumes, precision, and mesmerizing routines make them a highlight of halftime shows and marching band competitions.

Color guard requires rhythm, grace, and concentration. Coordination and well-honed technique are absolutely necessary for carrying out a dazzling performance. The performers must be able to move together fluidly to complete a routine successfully. Color guard is sometimes called

Sometimes, a marching band's show design positions some members of the band front behind the musicians during a parade, as seen in this 2003 Rose Parade performance by the Homestead High School Spartan Alliance Band from Fort Wayne, Indiana.

the "sport of the arts" because it borrows and uses many movements from both athletics and dance. Flashy costumes, intricate dance steps, and elaborate flag work must all complement the music. Choreographers for the color guard work closely with band directors to plan a performance, creating a fitting visual counterpart to the band's music.

Costumes and makeup are chosen with care for each routine. The main piece of color guard equipment is a flag attached to a five- or six-foot-long (1.5 or 1.8 meters) pole, but members also work other props.

Flags of varying sizes are brought into shows, as are mock weapons such as rifles and sabers. Flag colors change depending on the specific routine, while the mock rifles—which are made of wood—are painted to complement costumes and flags. Long, diaphanous, colored streamers are also sometimes used to accentuate the group's movements. The flags, and by extension the color guards themselves, are often called silks.

Pom Squads

Marching band shows may include dazzling routines by the pom squad. Although most are independent groups that also perform for a variety of other events, pom squads add an extra touch of excitement and showmanship to marching band performances.

Pom squads incorporate both dance and cheerleading techniques in their routines. Members, sometimes called "pommers," must master dance steps such as pirouettes, leaps, and axels, as well as learn chants and cheer motions. Pom routines are often complicated and fast-paced, requiring confidence and solid memorization. Teamwork is essential to an effective pom squad. Members work together as they change formations and coordinate precise moves with perfect timing. The trademark of a pom squad, of course, are the fluffy pom pons waved throughout routines.

Groups perform in a variety of styles to different kinds of music. Pom squad members often have experience in ballet, jazz, or hip-hop dance. Some pom squads choreograph their own dance routines, giving

A pom squad puts hard work into coordinating moves and honing a routine until it's perfect. To the crowd, though, the pommers' most important quality is their enthusiasm.

members a chance to experiment with putting their ideas for moves and themes into action.

Fans at a halftime show or parade probably don't fully appreciate the amount of dedication required to prepare a truly impressive pom performance. Pom squad members must stay in shape and attend long hours of practice to hone their skills. It takes a lot of hard work for a group to make their routines look fun and natural. But once the pom squad is in the spotlight, with the marching band playing in the

A twirler shows off her skills during the All American halftime show of the Capital One Bowl in Orlando, Florida. A twirling routine includes dance moves as well as twirling and tossing the baton.

background and a cheering crowd in front of them, the experience is well worth the effort.

Majorettes

Have you ever tried to twirl a baton? You have probably at least toyed with a baton a few times, perhaps even managing to spin it through a couple of jerky revolutions before dropping it on the floor. Baton twirling is the most basic skill required of majorettes, the twirlers of the band front. The baton is the focus of flashy routines in which majorettes strut and wheel on the field in time to the music.

Majorettes twirl batons to music during a marching band's production number, performed after the band takes the field and forming the heart of the show. During their performance, they twirl their batons

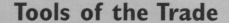

Tools of the Trade

Color guards work with many props, from mock weapons to streamers. Their most important props are their flags, which come in a wide variety of types and sizes. The regular flag is usually about 5 feet (1.5 m) long and 3 feet (0.9 m) wide and has stoppers at both ends of a stiff pole. A swing flag is similar to a regular flag, except the staff has only enough room to be gripped by one hand. On a chain flag, a metal chain threads through the silk, allowing the user to wrap it around his or her body. Half-and-half flags have poles made out of metal and plastic piping. The piping gives the pole more drag as it moves through the air, which makes it somewhat harder to twirl. On a butterfly flag, the silk is attached to both ends of the pole, with space left to grip it in the middle. Twirling a butterfly flag can give the effect of twirling two flags at once.

Batons come in many sizes to accommodate a variety of arm lengths and preferences. The ideal baton should be approximately the length of the twirler's arm, as measured from the underarm to the tip of the middle finger. They are made of a variety of materials, from lightweight aluminum and plastic to heavier wood and stainless steel. Standard batons have rubber stoppers at each end. Ribbon batons have ribbons at each end. Lighted batons feature ends that act as flashlights and can appear quite dramatic in a blacked-out room or on a darkened field. Hoop batons are essentially hula hoops with a baton running through the center.

through complicated routines while marching in complex patterns. Majorettes often wear striking uniforms and march with a high step—known as "the strut"—that involves lifting the leg about 12 inches (30.4 cm) into the air at the knee while keeping in step with other team members. Balance, timing, and coordination are key. Majorettes often train in dance schools before becoming part of a group.

In the past, majorettes were often the only female members of a marching band. Many bands of the mid-twentieth century were led by majorettes. As marching bands have evolved and women have become involved in other aspects of the bands, the majorette's role has shifted to bolstering the band's production number. Today, many majorettes prefer to be called twirlers, though not all twirlers are majorettes or involved in marching bands.

Twirling has become a popular and highly competitive activity. In addition to performing in the band front, majorettes often perform in twirling competitions. Many national competitions are held every year for majorettes. These events showcase the skill and precision required to twirl the baton. As more people participate in twirling and progress to advanced levels, new twirls and difficult techniques have been introduced in routines. Today, twirling requires far more athletic ability than ever before.

Drum Majors

The drum major may be one of the most important nonplaying members of the band. Unlike most other members of the band front, the

One of the most visible figures in a marching band, the drum major provides commands to the musicians during performances. The drum major must memorize long passages of music.

drum major must be a leader as well as a team player. He or she must possess a high level of musicianship and earn the respect of other band members.

The drum major's main responsibilities are to warm up the band before practices and conduct during performances. Drum majors work closely with band members and leaders to organize and direct shows and programs. They also help train new members in marching fundamentals, work with band section leaders to organize rehearsals, and help the director run drills. They help to motivate the band by keeping a positive attitude through long rehearsals and setting a good example.

During performances, drum majors can either lead the band independently or act as auxiliary leaders for an on-field conductor. The number of drum majors on the field may vary depending on the size of the band. Small bands may require only one, while larger bands need several to keep a musical program running smoothly.

It is vital that the drum major has a firm grasp of both the marching program and the music. Even when acting under the direction of a main conductor, the drum majors lead band sections and must keep them coordinated with other sections. The drum major must also be aware of the other members of the band front, such as the color guard, and work to keep the visual aspect of a show running as seamlessly as the music itself. This is especially important with large bands, which can have more than 500 members. When leading the band on the field, the drum majors must be as visible to other members as possible. They often use props such as batons or glow sticks to conduct.

Skills and Making the Team

Each member of the band front must be able to carry out his or her part in the performance, using skills and knowledge acquired through long hours of practice and rehearsal. Though the band front's sections differ from each other, many of the skills required to take part are similar. Physical fitness, coordination, and balance are important for any band front member. For all sections, dedication,

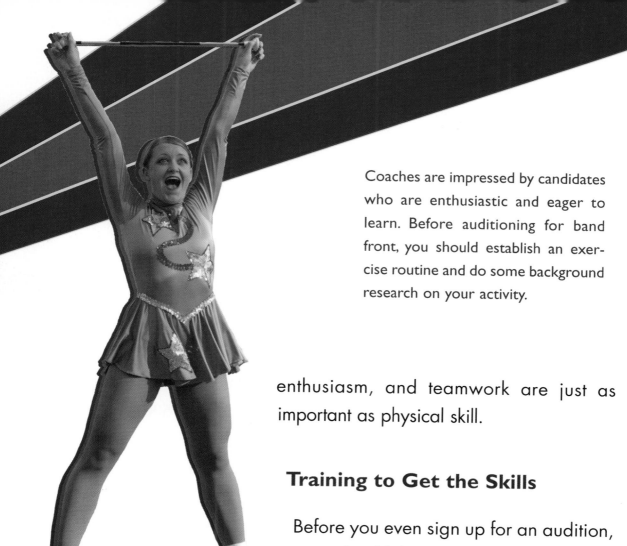

Coaches are impressed by candidates who are enthusiastic and eager to learn. Before auditioning for band front, you should establish an exercise routine and do some background research on your activity.

enthusiasm, and teamwork are just as important as physical skill.

Training to Get the Skills

Before you even sign up for an audition, you should learn everything you can about your activity and familiarize yourself with some of the basic moves. If you're new to band front, your coach or band director will not expect you to have already mastered the advanced skills. He or she will look for candidates who are well prepared, enthusiastic, and eager to learn and improve their routines.

Far in advance of the tryouts, you should take care to exercise regularly and eat a healthful diet so that you will be in good shape for rigorous practices when you make the team. If you participate in dance or gymnastics, devote some extra time to moves that may cross over into color guard or twirling routines. Practice with friends, too. They may offer you helpful hints, keep you from getting discouraged, and give you a chance to accustom yourself to working as part of a team.

Flag Skills

When practicing to audition for a color guard, two of the most important words to keep in mind at all times are "up" and "down." These refer to the positions of the flag's top and bottom and can help you keep your rhythm while practicing basic flag positions. Before auditioning or putting together a routine, you should familiarize yourself with several basic positions that are standard to color guard routines.

In the right shoulder position, the left hand is curled around the flag's stopper and set in the navel. The right hand grips the flag just above the head. The flag is held vertically about 3 inches (7.6 cm) from the nose, while the head is held at a 45-degree angle. The right shoulder position is the starting point for most flag positions. Front present position requires that the left hand maintain its grip from the right shoulder position, while pushing outward with the right hand and locking the arm. In the back present position, the performer does just the opposite from the front present position: the right hand stays in place close to the body, while the left hand pushes outward from the body, parallel to the ground, until the arm locks.

Right present and left present involve bringing the flag over to one or the other side while keeping the left hand at the navel. The horizontal

Color guard members at Franklin Central High School in Indianapolis, Indiana, spin their flags during a show. Advanced flag techniques include difficult spins and tosses.

position calls for the flag to be brought parallel to the eyes. Right slam and left slam require the flag to be brought down sharply on a diagonal toward the ground without letting it touch the grass.

Beginning color guard members also need to learn form—their position relative to others in a performing group. Members need to be aware of their teammates' positions at all times, whether marching or spinning flags or other equipment.

Twirling Skills

If you want to become a majorette, you might want to check out a video on basic twirling techniques. You could also sign up for a group twirling class or private lessons with a coach. Either of these options will help familiarize you with a few basic twirls and the strut.

Twirling requires precise hand-eye coordination as well as general coordination and balance of movement. Routines generally include a variety of different twirls, tosses, and dance steps. A majorette must shift fluidly from one move to the next with grace and carefully controlled precision. This is especially important when twirling in formation with a group.

Advanced twirling includes techniques such as arm and leg rolls, two-handed spins, difficult throws, intricate dance steps, and twirling two or even three batons. Three-baton twirling requires that the majorette simultaneously juggle and twirl the batons. Twirling is increasingly being recognized as a demanding sport, and individual routines for competitions involve a series of choreographed maneuvers equivalent to a full-body workout.

A twirler can also incorporate eye-catching novelty props into a routine. The fire baton emits real flames from its tips. The Samoan dance sword and the Samoan fire knife are used in routines derived from traditional Samoan dances, in which the sword or knife is spun using techniques similar to baton twirls. Needless to say, these variations are not recommended for beginners!

An accomplished majorette, such as this fire baton twirler, may be featured as the star performer at a halftime show. Many champion twirlers began baton twirling at a very young age.

Selecting a Drum Major

Drum majors are often among the hardest-working people in a marching band. They carry a great deal of responsibility in rehearsals and in performance. Unlike other band front positions, drum majors are usually not chosen through auditions or tryouts. The marching band itself usually chooses drum majors by election. Once elected, the drum majors become the student leaders of the band. The position cannot be taken lightly, as it calls for working hard and coordinating practices and performances with both the band instructor and the band members.

Team Tryouts

No matter how well you have trained, your band front future depends on your performance at team tryouts. In addition to learning the basic skills for color guard or twirling, you should mentally prepare yourself for tryouts. They test a candidate's ability to perform well under pressure, which is crucial considering that the band front will take part in shows in front of huge crowds. Coaches also take into account a candidate's attitude and ability to learn quickly.

The night before tryouts begin, you should get together everything that you will need for the next day. Lay out your clothes, pack a bag with bottled water and a snack, and read over any audition information one last time. Make sure that you have filled out any forms and assembled

Drum majors are generally elected by the band. Before the election, band members nominate potential candidates who possess a high degree of musical ability and leadership qualities. This band's two drum majors (in front) high strut as they lead the musicians in parade.

any paperwork that you might need to take with you. Go to bed early so that you will be well rested for tryouts.

Take care with your appearance, but keep your makeup light. Tie back your hair and wear comfortable, well-fitting clothes so that the coach can judge your form. Arrive early to the tryouts so that you won't have to rush onto the floor.

Every candidate feels jittery before tryouts, no matter his or her level of experience. Combat nerves with a positive attitude. Remember that your coach and peers want to see you succeed. If you make a mistake, don't dwell on it! Focus on the positive aspects of your performance, and concentrate on doing your best on the next move.

Some tryouts last a few days. The coach may require that candidates learn and rehearse a new routine. Try to make a tape of the routine music so that you can practice on your own. Also, don't be afraid to ask questions or request help.

Throughout the tryouts, keep in mind the importance of showmanship and enthusiasm. Move with confidence and never stop smiling. The coach is looking for candidates who will raise spirit in a cheering crowd of fans. Even if you lack experience, a positive mind-set and an ability to pick up a new routine quickly will make a good impression.

Making a Commitment

Once you make the team, the hard work of being a band front member really begins. Most people see majorettes, the color guard, and the pom squad only at rallies and shows. Behind the scenes, the members put in long hours of preparation for performances and competitions.

When you join the band front, you are making a commitment to participate in every aspect of the team—whether it's practice, performances, or fund-raising—and to always put forth your best effort. The responsibilities of balancing band front, school, and other activities can seem daunting, especially to new members. You must learn to manage your time efficiently in order to succeed and enjoy band front. If you find that you are falling behind in your work or if you feel overwhelmed, talk to your coach, parents, or a school counselor.

Teamwork

A commitment to the band front is also a commitment to your teammates. Ideally, your teammates will be your close friends and supporters, but it takes work on the part of every member to build a close-knit team. Personality clashes and rivalries will emerge. If personal grudges start to interfere with the team's progress, every member must make a conscious effort to put the good of the team above individual differences.

Your coach or captain will not be impressed if you try to outshine your peers. It is important that you work on improving your own skills, but when you practice with your team, your job is to cooperate with your teammates.

A good relationship with your teammates can make band front a rewarding and memorable experience. Encouragement from your teammates can give you the confidence to excel beyond your own expectations. When you are feeling frustrated or discouraged, your team's enthusiasm can help raise your spirits. Even away from band front, your experience in working as a team will help in your schoolwork and in your dealings with family and friends.

CHAPTER 3

Practice

For every performance given by the band front, innumerable days must go into practice. Even members who have mastered the fundamental skills will have to learn how to perform more elaborate routines. They may have to accustom themselves to working with props or in uniform. Most important, they will have to learn to work with other team members and stay encouraged. Many groups even attend

At practices, band front members perfect the moves that will dazzle the crowd when performed as part of a choreographed routine.

camps to bond with each other, improve their skills, and learn new routines.

Team Practice

All aspects of band front call for team members to work well together. While some activities, such as twirling or flag work, can be practiced alone, teams have to practice together to present a flawless program. Practices can also be used to determine the strengths and weaknesses of individual team members. The captain can then assign roles according to each member's strengths, while offering extra help to overcome weak points.

Practice time and frequency often vary between teams and organizations. Some teams practice five days a week, while less intensive teams may practice only twice a week. Most middle school and high school teams schedule practice after school, when it is easier to organize transportation for everyone. Some teams, however, hold practices early in the mornings before school. Members of these teams often find themselves practicing before the sun rises. The length of practice sessions also varies. Two to three hours are normal, particularly for high school or middle school groups. Some college and professional groups practice for five or six hours, or even longer if a routine needs extra work.

Practices follow different patterns for each section of the band front. The drum majors spend time going over the music with the band leader, rehearsing different sections of the band, and marching with the band during practice runs. Majorettes work on various twirls and dance steps. The color guard practices its spins, steps, and holds. Pom squads work on their acrobatics and dance routines.

Most practice sessions start with stretching exercises to warm up muscles, followed by rehearsal of routines and intensive work on perfecting fundamental skills and learning more advanced techniques. Practices are usually accompanied by recorded music for all but the drum majors, who actually work with the band. Teams also review the choreography for upcoming shows and work through potential problems. Just before practice ends, members may run through another series of stretching exercises to help their bodies cool down and prevent soreness.

Members of a color guard stretch before competition to warm up muscles and reduce the chance of injury. Participation in color guard and other band front activities requires a high level of athleticism.

Team Spirit

Like sports teams, band front groups need team spirit and a sense of camaraderie. Working together through practices and performances over the course of a season builds these qualities. People learn to trust each other and believe in what they are doing. They gain confidence in the group as they see the different elements coming together to form a whole. This trust, confidence, and togetherness form the essence of team spirit. Performances go more smoothly if members are focused yet comfortable together. Moreover, the knowledge of working together toward a common goal can make practices seem more fun and exciting.

Team spirit is important to keep groups motivated and focused on their goals. For the band front, this means that each section must work well with the others. The color guard, majorettes, pom squad, drum majors, and the marching band itself should coordinate as a single unit. This is most easily accomplished when the individual leaders have the respect of their section members. Leaders should offer encouragement and only constructive criticism to other members. These members, in turn, should give their undivided attention and respect to their leaders.

Even the best routines and individual units can be undermined if there's strife within the group or if leaders are overly critical and controlling. Keeping a positive attitude and working hard to make the team better should be everyone's main focus. After all, these are team activities, and all energy should go toward improving the team.

Uniforms and Costumes

Band front sections all have distinctive costumes designed to catch the spectators' eyes. Sections that incorporate flags or batons into their programs generally avoid baggy or flowing clothing, which can interfere with their props. Majorettes usually wear stylized versions of the marching band's uniforms, with tailed, tight-fitting jackets and skirts that stop just above the knee. Their high white boots accentuate their strut. They often

Color guards typically incorporate striking costumes, eye-catching props, and choreographed dance moves into their routines. The Hoover High School color guard of Hoover, Alabama, presents a spectacular routine with its long, brightly colored capes at the Rose Parade Band Fest on December 31, 2005.

use different uniforms depending on the show. Drum majors also wear some version of the band's uniform, often distinguished by cords or capes.

Color guards wear tight uniforms, usually consisting of leotards, jumpsuits, and tights. They sometimes use capes or scarves to accentuate their movements. Their costumes often change with their routines. Pom squads wear cheerleading uniforms featuring the school colors. Their uniforms may vary depending on whether they are performing at a home or away game. Some pom squads reserve special uniforms for competitions.

Each band front group generally tries to coordinate hairstyles and makeup. Majorettes and color guard members tend to pull their hair back to keep it out of the way of props. Pom squad members may wear their hair down, teased out, and sprayed firmly in place. (Big hair makes a good impression when seen from a distance by a large crowd.) Makeup must be carefully applied so that it will not streak after a strenuous routine. Eyes and lips are generally accentuated. When properly applied, bold touches such as masks of color or simple designs painted on the face can create a dramatic effect. Some college and professional groups engage professional hairstylists and makeup consultants.

Handling Props

One of the first lessons band front members learn is to take great care in handling props. A respect for props becomes second nature to band front members. Dropping or fumbling flags, batons, poms, or mock weapons can throw off an individual's timing and may interfere with or even injure other members. During competitions, points are deducted for dropping props.

Majorettes often practice twirling for years before they join a squad, learning to twirl without dropping the baton from an early age. Pom squad members have to keep the motions of their pom pons perfectly coordinated to create a striking impression from a distance. Color guard members learn precise movements and spacing to keep their flags from striking other members. They learn never to let the flag touch the ground during a routine.

Only advanced members handle the rifles and sabers, which are dulled and often taped to prevent injury. When practices or performances end, the props are cleaned and carefully stored so that they will be ready for use the next day. Damaged flags, weapons, and batons are set aside for repair or to be used exclusively in practice.

Going to Camp

Training camps usually take place in the summer to give band front sections additional training in the pageantry arts. Camps often last for one to two weeks and are usually held on college campuses, where campers stay in dorm rooms until the camp ends. Schools usually make the camps voluntary. Some camps take all members of the band front and hold separate classes for each section. Others focus exclusively on one section of the band front. Still other camps include the entire marching band.

Training at camp is often intense, usually lasting eight hours a day with scheduled breaks. Typically, mornings are spent learning and reviewing basic fundamentals. After lunch, campers spend the afternoon working through routines to prerecorded music with expert instructors. Students wanting extra instruction can usually train one-on-one with instructors in special sessions after everyone else finishes for the day. Games and contests are sometimes held during lessons to encourage campers and make the training fun. After the day's instructions, camps usually hold social events such as dances, games, talent shows, and contests that allow campers to mingle with each other and make new friends.

Members of the color guard section of Salem High School's Blue Devil marching band fine-tune their flag-handling skills during band camp on August 17, 2005. Each year, the Salem, New Hampshire, band holds a two-week camp prior to the opening of school to work on routines for football season.

Band front members often come away from camp with new perspectives on their sport and their teammates. Members who barely knew each other outside of practice and performances may form strong bonds after spending most of every day with each other. The intense classes and workouts serve to hone skills. Campers learn new dance steps or different ways to approach a familiar routine from instructors and teams from other schools. Most important, they often gain new confidence in themselves and in their teammates.

CHAPTER
4

Performance Opportunities

Weeks of practice and rehearsals ultimately pay off when the band front performs in front of an audience. Jangling nerves are forgotten as the captains bring their sections forward and the routine begins. Each participant is lost in the moment, moving fluidly with the rest of the team through steps perfected during long hours of drills. Teams work for weeks on choreography and technique in

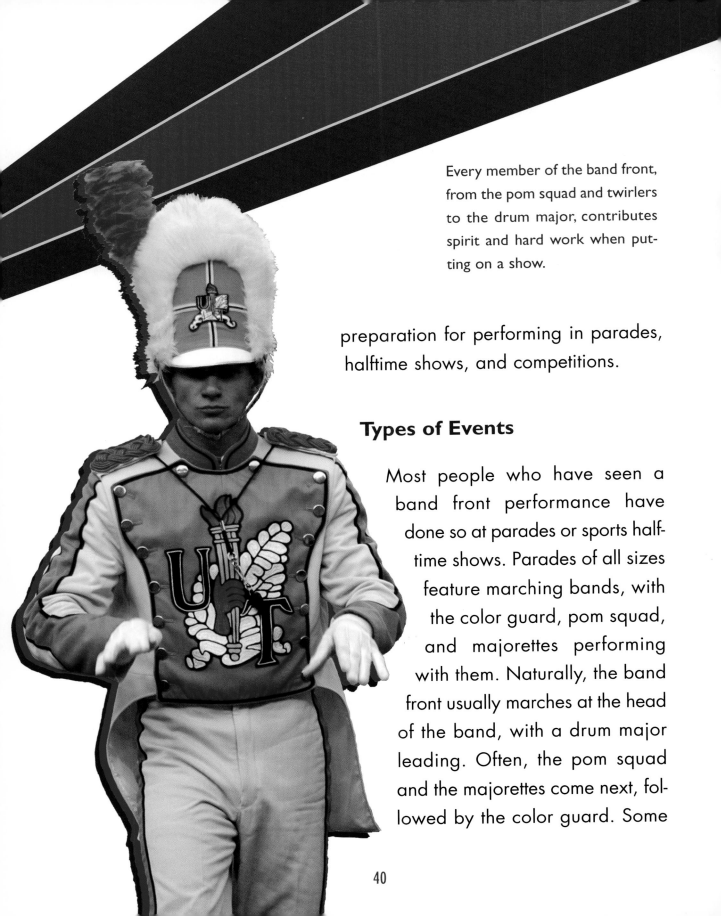

Every member of the band front, from the pom squad and twirlers to the drum major, contributes spirit and hard work when putting on a show.

preparation for performing in parades, halftime shows, and competitions.

Types of Events

Most people who have seen a band front performance have done so at parades or sports halftime shows. Parades of all sizes feature marching bands, with the color guard, pom squad, and majorettes performing with them. Naturally, the band front usually marches at the head of the band, with a drum major leading. Often, the pom squad and the majorettes come next, followed by the color guard. Some members may carry a wide banner between them proclaiming the name of the school or band. The band front members' routines are choreographed to move to the music played by the rest of the band.

The pom squads in particular play a major role at pep rallies to boost school spirit before an athletic event. Often framed by the color guard, they perform elaborate acrobatic routines while cheering for the team. They form lines and dance, sometimes stacking themselves in human pyramids while waving their poms in unison and chanting cheers. The color guard joins in, presenting their flags while the band plays. If the school sponsors a majorette team, the twirlers also perform routines.

Sometimes all sections of the band front are on the floor together, presenting a dazzling spectacle to energize the crowd. In other cases, they take the floor separately to perform their routines at intervals punctuated by an emcee and the band. The band front performs in full costume with all of the props that they will use during the halftime show. They smile throughout, conveying their enthusiasm for the team and for their own performance. Audiences may get brief previews of the night's halftime show or of the band front's competition routines.

Halftime shows are the most spectacular school-sponsored events, usually held at football and basketball games. A show is designed so that the band front complements the band's music. Music is often chosen to reflect a unifying theme. The band front performs its routines as the band plays through the theme music. Movie themes are popular, ranging from classics like *West Side Story* or *The Wizard of Oz* to more recent films like *Chicago*. Other themes may draw on music by pop acts, such as the Beatles,

Though spectators might be struck by the performers' spontaneous enthusiasm, an effective performance is the product of careful preparation. Each element is planned and rehearsed in advance, from the overall theme down to choreographic details.

or the works of classical composers. The music of American composers George Gershwin and Leonard Bernstein are popular choices for half-time themes because the narrative quality of their music adapts easily to visual interpretation.

Competitions

Band front competitions are usually held from spring to fall, during the marching season. The performances in these contests between schools

Winter Guard

The onset of winter doesn't have to mean an end to band front activity. When the marching season ends, color guards often move indoors to become the winter guard. Winter guards share much in common with color guards. Both groups perform choreographed routines set to music while using flags and other props. Unlike color guards, winter guards cannot exceed thirty guard members and musicians combined. Most winter guards use prerecorded music, though some continue to work with the band. Their costumes and routines are often more elaborate than those of the color guard, and a greater emphasis is placed on theatrical staging. Winter guards compete against each other in local, regional, and national competitions sponsored by organizations such as Winter Guard International.

are often long and strenuous. Team members draw on the stamina they've built through practice and their confidence in their own abilities to compete successfully.

Competitions take place between local, regional, and national teams. The competition season for color guards usually begins with local events held in February, when teams have had months to work together and perfect their routines. Events take place on weekends. By April, teams will have advanced to regional and national competitions.

The Arcadia High School marching band takes the field at the Arcadia Festival of Bands in Arcadia, California. Eye-catching costumes and imaginative choreography bring excitement to the color guard's performance.

Pom squads and majorettes begin competing in early fall, with regionals held in late winter and national competitions wrapping up in April. The two largest baton-twirling associations in the United States—the United States Twirling Association (USTA) and the National Baton Twirling Association (NBTA)—each hold competitions every year for majorettes. Winners of the NBTA's Junior and Senior Men's, Women's, and Team divisions then go on to compete at the world championships, held annually by the World Baton Twirling Federation (WBTF).

Teams compete in a variety of categories depending on the group's size and experience level. Competitions featuring entire marching bands often have separate categories for each section of the band front, as well as the main contest. Competition categories also exist for small groups, pairs, and individuals. Organizations such as Marching Auxiliaries, which conducts ten regional championship events throughout the United States, hold sectional contests in the same location over one weekend. The biggest of these events is the Bands of America Grand National Championship, held every November at the RCA Dome in Indianapolis.

Groups are judged on costumes, equipment, movement, dance interpretation, and overall effect before the final scores are added and the winners announced. Every performance detail should be flawless during a competition, from choreography to makeup.

Criteria for competition and judging are often rigid. Marching band competitions have report times—usually ten minutes into the previous band's performance—when they must be at the starting gate. They are assigned step-off times, designating exactly when they should take the field to perform. Fifteen minutes is a standard length for a competition performance. Bands are given very strict space limitations and can be penalized when members step out of the performance area. They are also instructed on where to enter and leave the field. Contests are intended to run smoothly, so bands are penalized for going under the minimum or over the maximum competition times. Costumes and equipment need to meet competition standards. Rules also exist prohibiting certain types of props. Using fire or animals is often forbidden.

Preparing: What to Expect

One minute you're standing with your teammates at the gate, equipment at hand and steeling yourself to march. Perhaps you're going over the routine in your head or thinking about the long bus ride that brought your group to the competition. The next minute you're on the field or floor and working through the program. You may be aware of the crowd's eyes on you, or you may be so deep into your performance that you barely notice anyone other than your teammates. You'll probably see the judges, though, who will likely be sitting at the front of the performance space, often on risers so that they can observe the whole show.

The judges are usually past participants in the events that they evaluate. They take part in frequent mandatory workshops to keep themselves up to date on requirements and criteria. The National Judges Association is an organization that dedicates itself to educating and improving its members in judging pageantry competitions. The organization certifies qualified members to judge competitions in cheerleading, color guard, twirling, and parades. Qualified members are also certified for judging large national competitions, such as the Tournament of Bands, at national, state, and local levels.

When your group performs, the judges refer to diagrams of the choreographed routine to see how closely it is followed. They make deductions when they see mistakes and take the group's successes into account when tabulating the score. Winners and prizes are announced after the last group performs.

A well-choreographed color guard routine incorporates flashy moves and smooth transitions. Guard members must move in perfect synchronization with the band's music.

Winning and Losing

Competition winners receive awards ranging from medals and trophies to scholarships. Medals are given for first through fourth place. When the band front sections are part of a marching band competition, the points from their scores are added to points from other sections. The totals for the whole band are tabulated and trophies are awarded for first through third place, with additional awards going to the best in each section.

The Heritage High School drum major and color guard captain accept the second-place trophy for their band at the Indiana State School Music Association (ISSMA) state marching band championships.

Awards vary among the sections of the band front. Some pom squad, color guard, and majorette competitions offer scholarships to winners, as well as trophies or medals. Awards may also go to individual members or people who chose to compete as individuals. Some competitions may break awards down to categories, such as best costumes or best choreography.

Winners are more respected and appreciated by coaches, judges, and other teams if they accept their awards with grace and good sportsmanship. Those who do not win earn the respect of other teams if they graciously accept their scores and congratulate the winners. They might go over their scores to see where they need improvement. Every group should focus on its positive achievements, whether it's an improved score from previous years, a success on a troublesome aspect of its routine, or simply the knowledge that it worked hard and did its best.

CHAPTER
5

Band Front and You

Becoming a member of the band front can by turns be exciting, invigorating, frustrating, exhausting, and fun. Practicing and performing routines can give members new confidence. Months of working out and exercising improve physical conditioning. Exceptional performers can even work toward scholarships and career opportunities. Learning to ride with the ups and downs of the marching and competition seasons

Participation in band front may easily be one of the highlights of your school year, but balancing band front responsibilities with academic work and other activities can be a challenge.

builds patience and character. Teamwork and good sportsmanship can lead to rewarding and enduring friendships.

Keeping in Tune with Your Body

Band front is both an artistic and an athletic activity. Majorettes twirl, pom squads perform acrobatics, and the color guard presents and spins its equipment. All three groups incorporate dance into their routines. Regular practices and performances require strength and stamina. Members need to keep themselves in shape, yet they also need to be aware of physical limitations.

Pressing yourself too hard can lead to physical fatigue and injury. Instead, remember to relax and take it easy on days when you're not at your physical best.

A number of factors go into keeping your body functioning well. Eating right and getting plenty of sleep keeps you physically and mentally sharp for practice. Regular aerobic exercise and cross-training keep muscles strong and build endurance. Stretching before and after practice prevents soreness and keeps your body limber. Knowing your limits and easing off when you feel that you're reaching them can help avoid injury and keep you healthy and at your peak performance level.

Staying Healthy

Staying healthy through practices, events, and competition can be difficult when band front events must be coordinated with school and other extracurricular activities. Some band front teams strongly discourage members from other sports and athletic activities. Taking on too many sports can drain away energy and focus from the color guard, the pom squad, or a majorette team. Teams usually have academic requirements as well. A team member in danger of failing may be too worried or stressed out to concentrate on learning routines.

A healthful diet is just as important in the band front as in any other sport. The body needs calories to burn during exercise, as well as vitamins and minerals to keep physical functions in tune. Members should eat full, well-balanced meals heavy in carbohydrates to keep up the needed energy. Fruits and vegetables, as well as breads, pasta, and grains, are excellent foods for athletes because they are high in carbohydrates and low in fat. Dairy products are necessary to build strong bones. It's a common myth that the lactose found in dairy foods causes muscle soreness and fatigue. To the contrary, it can actually delay fatigue during performance.

Drinking plenty of water while exercising is as important as good nutrition. As you exercise, you lose water through perspiration. Losing too much water leads to dehydration and can result in dizziness or illness. Drink water when you feel you need it, but try not to drink too much. Otherwise, you may cramp up or feel ill.

Most school-sponsored athletic programs require members to get physicals before they are allowed to participate. Doctors check your heart rate, breathing, reflexes, vision, and hearing before letting you know that you've passed. If you notice changes in your breathing, heart rate, or some other physical function, schedule another examination right away. Ignoring a possible health condition can be disastrous to you and the team.

Avoiding Injuries

Injuries are common to every sport and can happen to even the best athletes. Pulled muscles, sprains, and more serious conditions could force you to sit out practices or even leave the team. One of the most basic ways to avoid injury to muscles and ligaments is to stretch regularly before and after practice. This not only prevents soreness, it also improves your flexibility. Stretching gives you the ability to move better and more fluidly, improving your range of motion and your overall performance.

Top band front members keep themselves in excellent physical shape. Stretching and cross-training exercises can boost performance in band front routines and reduce the likelihood of injuries.

Stretching can seem tedious and painful, especially if you are already sore from the previous day. It's tempting to rush through stretches to get on with practices and workouts, but they should be done properly. Twenty to thirty minutes of stretching is recommended before exercise. Stretches should encompass a wide range of muscle movement in the arms, legs, back, and torso. Be sure to hold each stretch for twenty to thirty seconds. Because band front requires flexibility in both the upper and lower body, you should concentrate on both areas.

Stretching is most effective when you follow a set routine, beginning with light exercise such as toe touches or windmills, followed by stationary stretches where the body is at rest. Ankles, hamstrings, calves, and the groin can be stretched by placing stress on the muscle and holding it. Many programs follow this with motion stretches, in which the body or extremities are turned to loosen them up. This is effective with abdominal and back muscles. The same stretches can be repeated after exercising to cool down.

Avoiding injury also requires knowing your physical limitations and avoiding risks. Sudden, unaccustomed movement can seriously damage muscles and ligaments. Instead, you should gradually build up to more elaborate or strenuous routines, giving your body time to get accustomed to the necessary motions. If a movement causes sudden pain, you should stop and have it examined by a doctor or trainer. Pressing on despite the pain can turn a minor injury into a major one that may end your days in the band front. Take care to follow the doctor's instructions and take it easy until the injury has healed.

Cross-Training

Because of the wide range of movement required for color guards, pom squads, and majorettes, a great deal of muscle strength is required. The upper body and arms must be strong to work with flags, twirl batons, and boost teammates overhead. Dance steps and constant motion require endurance. Many band front teams do cross-training exercises to gain and increase strength and endurance. Cross-training refers to a combination of two or more types of exercise designed to boost overall physical performance. Dancing and jogging are excellent ways to build endurance and stamina. Teams may lift weights to increase upper-body strength in the arms, shoulders, and torso.

Cross-training works best when strength exercises and stamina exercises are done on alternating days. Teams might lift weights two days a week and devote the other three to stamina, or vice versa. When cross-training, it's important to remember not to overdo the exercises, which can lead to diminished performance through fatigue. One benefit of cross-training is that it allows one muscle group to rest while the other is exercised.

Keeping in Shape

Remaining fit and healthy is easiest when following an established routine. Exercise eventually becomes a habit. To remain in shape, you should continue exercising during the off-season. Taking up another sport during the off-season is a good way to stay in shape. Many communities offer summer programs, especially for middle school and high school students. Gymnastics and dance classes can help improve form and technique. Endurance can be maintained by taking part in league swimming competitions or running events and bicycle races.

Your Future

Graduating from high school doesn't have to mean the end of participating in the band front. Colleges and universities often have color guard, pom squad, and majorette programs as extracurricular activities. Schools with large athletic programs actively recruit skilled band

Whether you're performing at a halftime show or a national competition, your most important job in band front is to have a good time raising spirit before a cheering crowd.

front members to present spectacular halftime shows. The University of South Florida, for example, offers scholarships for color guard members who maintain an A average in band class.

Band front organizations also award college scholarships to outstanding band front members. The Michigan Color Guard Circuit (MCGC) awards fifteen to twenty scholarships annually. Some major twirling competitions award scholarships as first prizes. The National Baton Twirling Association, the largest sanctioned baton twirling organization in the United States, holds its annual competition in South Bend, Indiana. The 2001 winner, Julie Canterbury, walked away with nearly $1,000 in scholarships.

The dance and theatrical skills mastered in band front can prove useful in many career paths, even if you decide not to continue participating in college. A background in band front is handy for majors in dance, music, or theater. Sports-related fields, such as physical education, physical therapy, or even psychology may also be a good fit. Many theme parks also showcase band front groups as entertainment. Community-based color guards and pom squads often make appearances at parades and special events.

Even if your interests take you in an entirely different direction, you will still have the important lessons and fond memories from your life in band front. The ability to work well with others as part of a team is a key to success in many careers. Following routines and working methodically toward a goal despite obstacles will bring you rewards in both your personal and professional life. Giving your best, keeping up enthusiasm, and feeling good about a goal teaches you not to dwell on the past but to look ahead to the future.

Glossary

axel (or axel turn) A type of dance move.

baton A slender, tapered rod used to conduct an orchestra; a hollow metal rod with stoppers on both ends that is twirled by a drum major or majorette.

charisma Personal magnetism or charm that commands the admiration or loyalty of others.

choreography The artistic arrangement of movement in dance.

color guard A flag corps attached to a marching band.

conductor The leader of a band or other musical group.

majorette A baton twirler who accompanies a marching band.

pageantry A term referring to performances by ensembles that evolved in part from military displays, such as marching band, color guard, and drum majorettes.

pirouette A rapid whirling of the body, especially performed in dance.

procession A group of individuals moving forward in an orderly and often formal manner.

regimental Belonging to or pertaining to a regiment, or military unit.

routine A rehearsed dance or theatrical number.

saber (or sabre) A type of sword.

stamina Physical endurance.

For More Information

Drum Corps International (DCI)
470 South Irmen Drive
Addison, IL 60101
(630) 628-7888
e-mail: dci@dci.org
Web site: http://www.dci.org

Drum Majorettes of America
c/o Doris Faber, Executive Director
P.O. Box 19028
Charlotte, NC 28219
(704) 392-5472
e-mail: dfaber2520@aol.com
Web site: http://www.dmatwirl.org

United States Twirling Association
44 Drexel Drive
Bay Shore, NY 11706
(631) 961-0499
e-mail: executivedirector@ustwirling.com
Web site: http://www.ustwirling.com

Winter Guard International
7755 Paragon Road, Suite 104
Dayton, OH 45459
(937) 434-7100
e-mail: office@wgi.org
Web site: http://www.wgi.org

Web Sites

Due to the changing nature of Internet links, the Rosen Publishing Group, Inc., has developed an online list of Web sites related to the subject of this book. This site is updated regularly. Please use this link to access the list:

http://www.rosenlinks.com/team/bafr

For Further Reading

Coachman, Frank. *Marching Bands* (Team Spirit!). New York, NY: The Rosen Publishing Group, 2007.

Coachman, Mary Kaye. *Dance Team* (Team Spirit!). New York, NY: The Rosen Publishing Group, 2007.

McGahey, Susan. *Winter Guard* (Team Spirit!). New York, NY: The Rosen Publishing Group, 2007.

Nathan, Amy. *The Young Musician's Survival Guide: Tips from Teens and Pros*. New York, NY: Oxford University Press, 2000.

Sloan, Karyn. *Techniques of Color Guard*. Philadelphia, PA: Mason Crest Publishers, Inc., 2003.

Usilton, Terry. *Color Guard Competition*. Philadelphia, PA: Mason Crest Publishers, Inc., 2003.

Wheelus, Doris. *Baton Twirling: A Complete Illustrated Guide*. New York, NY: Lion Books, 1975.

Bibliography

Atwater, Constance. *Baton Twirling: The Fundamentals of an Art and a Skill*. Rutland, VT: Charles E. Tuttle Company, 1972.

Dunnigan, Patrick. *Marching Band Techniques*. Northfield, IL: The Instrumentalist Publishing Company, 1998.

Hanson, Mary Ellen. *Go! Fight! Win!: Cheerleading in American Culture*. Bowling Green, OH: Bowling Green State University Popular Press, 1995.

Holston, Kim R. *The Marching Band Handbook*. 3rd ed. Jefferson, NC: McFarland & Company, Inc., 2004.

Robins, Gilbert. *Welcome to Our World: Realities of High School Students*. Thousand Oaks, CA: Corwin Press, Inc., 1998.

Wright, Al. *Marching Band Fundamentals*. New York, NY: Carl Fischer, Inc., 1963.

Index

About the Author

Jason Porterfield is a writer and researcher who lives in Chicago, Illinois. The appreciation he shows here for the discipline and spectacle of marching band routines is due in large part to his fond memories of watching his award-winning high school band—the Giles High School Marching Spartans of Pearisburg, Virginia—perform on many occasions.

Series Consultant: Susan Epstein

Photo Credits

Cover © Kevin Fleming/Corbis; title page, pp. 8, 20, 30, 38, 50 Bruce Preston; pp. 5, 7, 12, 35, 42, 44, 47, 56 Dave Schaafsma, World of Pageantry Webmaster; p. 9 © James G. Pinsky/Getty Images; pp. 10, 23 Bob Bivens; p. 14 © Rudi Von Briel/Photo Edit; pp. 15, 21 © ESP Productions; p. 18 © Gary Connor/Photo Edit; p. 25 © Andy Lyons/Allsport/ Getty Images; p. 27 © Tom Carter/Photo Edit; p. 31 © Paul A. Souders/Corbis; p. 33 Ayala High School band and color guard, Chino Hills, CA, Mark Stone, director, photo by Jose A. Fernandez; pp. 39, 49 Frank Coachman; p. 40 © Elsa/Getty Images; p. 48 Bateman Photography; p. 53 © M. Möllenberg/zefa/Corbis.

Designer: Gene Mollica; Editor: Wayne Anderson; Photo Researcher: Marty Levick